Vintage

COSTUME
INSPIRATIONS

A RETRO LOOK-BOOK FEATURING OVER 100 MID-CENTURY COSTUMES

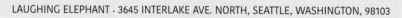

LAUGHING ELEPHANT · 3645 INTERLAKE AVE. NORTH, SEATTLE, WASHINGTON, 98103

ISBN/EAN: 9781514900314

LAUGHINGELEPHANT.com

PREFACE

Pretending, for a time, to be someone other than oneself through the use of masks, costume, makeup and other forms of disguise fulfills a deep psychological need. It offers us a brief vacation from our everyday identity. It refreshes us, as all vacations should, through an escape from our daily habits.

Contemporary society offers us few opportunities for disguise. We have Mardi Gras in New Orleans and elsewhere, also known as Carnival in Rio de Janiero, Venice and beyond. Masquerade parties, once very popular, are rare in the 21st century. Halloween remains as our main opportunity for disguise and costume–and while it was once the province of children, in recent years it has become a holiday for all ages.

We took the images in this book from European costume catalogs of the mid-twentieth century. We adore them for their imaginative variety and inspirational potential. Any object can be a costume! The manner in which the figures are mingled is both bizarre and delightful. At Halloween, one tends to see the same tired costumes year after year. This book, in its profusion, offers fresh paths and original thinking. We hope that its pages will inspire the costume seeker and that its users will soon attend balls, parties–or perhaps merely walk the streets–in the guise of ladybugs, atomic bombs, a donut, a high tension wire, or a box of chocolates.

Necktie

Confetti

Corn

Little Flower

The Vagabond

Bouquet

Spiral

Good Luck

Cleopatra

Orange

Mambo

Samba

Hawaiian Boy

Hawaiian Girl

Bell Girl

Chess Lady

Artist's Palette

Bouquet of Violets

Beetle

Gypsy

Butterfly
Hunter

Target

Ladybug

Blue Waltz

Dominos

Music

Madame
Chrysanthemum

Rabbit

Carrot

U.S.A.

The Milky Way

Scotsman

Greek Woman

Portuguese Lady

Hungarian Girl

Abbruzi Outlaw

Spanish Lady

Russian
Peasant

Peasant from
Montenegro

Straw Man

Lady of Hearts

Summer

Belladonna

Clown

Love's
Messenger

Saxon Lady

High Tension

Pilot

Flight
Attendant

Atomic
Bomb

Spiral

Robinson Crusoe

Horoscope

Carnation

Elephant

Chambermaid

Mermaid

Two-Face

Melody

Memory

Jazz

Rustic
Clown

Box of
Chocolate

Coral

Summer

Bullfighter

Moulin Rouge

Rosalinda

Surrealist

Pierette

Buffoon

Water Lily

Milliner

Fakir

Spaniard

Paris Gossip

Little Witch

Swiss Doll

Comet

Snow Lady

Dutch Girl

Sailor

Spanish
Dancer

Carnival Girl

Chianti

Squaw

Confetti

Sunflower

Chinese Toy

Empire Girl

Scottish Lass

Miss Universe

Cat

Carnival Fairy

Rider

Heart of Cherries

Martini

Cream
Pastry

Bowl of
Raspberries

Chianti

Espresso

Dutch Girl

Starry sky

Harem
Girl

Spinning Top

Puccinello

Telephone

Dutch
Girl

Lady Bug

Cherry

Dominos

Poppy

Vagabond

Chambermaid

Leopard

Chef

Magician

Donut

Mouse

Dutch Girl

Dutch Boy